A Look at Japan

by Helen Frost

Consulting Editor: Gail Saunders-Smith, Ph.D.

Consultant: Mark Ravina, Associate Professor, specializing in Japanese History Department of History, Emory University Atlanta, Georgia

Pebble Books

an imprint of Capstone Press
Mankato, Minnesota

Pebble Books are published by Capstone Press
1710 Roe Crest Drive, North Mankato, Minnesota 56003
www.capstonepub.com

Books published by Capstone Press are manufactured with paper
containing at least 10 percent post-consumer waste.

Library of Congress Cataloging-in-Publication Data
Frost, Helen, 1949–
    A look at Japan / by Helen Frost.
    p. cm.—(Our world)
    Includes bibliographical references (p. 23) and index.
    Summary: Simple text and photographs depict the land, animals, and people
of Japan.
    ISBN-13: 978-0-7368-1168-2 (hardcover)   ISBN-10: 0-7368-1168-0 (hardcover)
    ISBN-13: 978-0-7368-4857-2 (softcover)   ISBN-10: 0-7368-4857-6 (softcover)
    1. Japan—Pictorial works—Juvenile literature. [1. Japan.] I. Title. II. Our world
(Pebble Books)
DS806 .F76 2002
952—dc21   2001003308

The author thanks the children's section staff at the Allen County Public Library in
Fort Wayne, Indiana, for research assistance.

Note to Parents and Teachers

The Our World series supports national social studies standards related to
culture. This book describes and illustrates the land, animals, and people of
Japan. The photographs support early readers in understanding the text.
The repetition of words and phrases helps early readers learn new words.
This book also introduces early readers to subject-specific vocabulary
words, which are defined in the Words to Know section. Early readers may
need assistance to read some words and to use the Table of Contents,
Words to Know, Read More, Internet Sites, and Index/Word List sections of
the book.

Printed in the United States of America in North Mankato, Minnesota.
082012   006898

Table of Contents

Japan

★Tokyo

Japan is a country in eastern Asia. Japan has four main islands and many small islands. The capital of Japan is Tokyo.

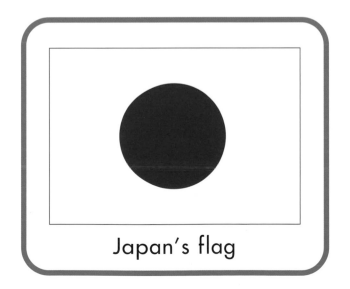

Japan's flag

coast

plains

forest

mountains

6

Japan has coasts, plains, forests, and mountains. Japan is colder in the north than it is in the south.

snow monkeys

sea lion

8

Snow monkeys, deer, and wild boars live in Japan's forests. Sea lions and turtles swim near Japan's coasts.

More than 126 million people live in Japan. Most people live in cities near the coasts. People in Japan speak Japanese. They use symbols to write this language.

hello	good-bye
今日は	さようなら
koh-NEE-chee-wah	sah-yoh-NAR-a

Rice, noodles, and fish are the main foods of Japan. Japanese people use chopsticks to eat.

Japanese people celebrate Children's Day on May 5. They hope for the health and happiness of all children on this day.

Japanese factory workers make cars, cameras, and video games to earn money. Farming and fishing also are important jobs in Japan.

Japan's money is counted in yen.

Japanese people travel by bike, car, bus, and train. Some trains travel so fast that they are called bullet trains.

Mount Fuji is the tallest mountain in Japan. Mount Fuji is a volcano. The last time it erupted was 1707.

Words to Know

chopsticks—two narrow sticks used to eat food; chopsticks are used mostly by people in Asian countries.

coast—land next to the sea

island—land surrounded by water; Japan has four main islands and many small islands.

language—the words and grammar that people use to talk and write to each other; the Japanese language is made up of symbols that stand for words and phrases.

plain—a large, flat area of land

snow monkey—a monkey that lives in Japan's mountains; snow monkeys have red faces; they also are called macaques.

Tokyo—the capital city of Japan; Tokyo is the largest city in Japan; more than 34 million people live in Tokyo.

volcano—a mountain with vents; Mount Fuji is a volcano in Japan; Mount Fuji is 12,387 feet (3,776 meters) above sea level.

Read More

Britton, Tamara L. *Japan*. The Countries. Edina, Minn.: Abdo Publishing, 2000.

Kalman, Bobbie. *Japan: The Culture*. Lands, Peoples, and Cultures Series. New York: Crabtree Publishing, 2001.

Sinnott, Susan. *Japan*. First Reports. Minneapolis: Compass Point Books, 2001.

Witherick, M. E. *Japan*. Country Studies. Chicago, Heinemann Library, 2000.

Internet Sites

FactHound offers a safe, fun way to find Internet sites related to this book. All of the sites on FactHound have been researched by our staff.

Here's all you do:

Visit *www.facthound.com*

FactHound will fetch the best sites for you!

Index/Word List

Asia, 5
bullet trains, 19
capital, 5
celebrate, 15
children, 15
Children's Day,
  15
chopsticks, 13
cities, 11
coasts, 7, 9, 11
country, 5
erupted, 21

farming, 17
fish, 13, 17
foods, 13
forests, 7, 9
happiness, 15
health, 15
islands, 5
jobs, 17
language, 11
live, 9, 11
money, 17
Mount Fuji, 21

mountain, 7, 21
people, 11,
  13, 15, 19
plains, 7
rice, 13
swim, 9
symbols, 11
Tokyo, 5
travel, 19
volcano, 21
workers, 17
write, 11

Word Count: 185
Early-Intervention Level: 17

Editorial Credits
Mari C. Schuh, editor; Kia Bielke, cover designer; Jennifer Schonborn, production
  designer and illustrator; Kimberly Danger and Alta Schaffer, photo researchers

Photo Credits
Betty Crowell, 14
Digital Stock, 1
Fritz Pölking/Visuals Unlimited, 8 (left)
International Stock/Miwako Ikeda, cover
Peter Essick/Aurora, 6 (lower right)
PhotoDisc, Inc., 8 (right), 20
Photo Network/Chad Ehlers, 6 (upper left), 10, 16
Prance/Visuals Unlimited, 6 (lower left)
Trip/N. Kealey, 6 (upper right); C. Rennie, 12; M. Fairman, 18